Zebras and Ostriches

By Kevin Cunningham

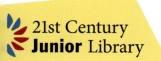

Published in the United States of America by
Cherry Lake Publishing
Ann Arbor, Michigan
www.cherrylakepublishing.com

Content Adviser: Stephen Ditchkoff, Professor of Wildlife Ecology and Management, Auburn University, Alabama
Reading Adviser: Marla Conn MS, Ed., Literacy specialist, Read-Ability, Inc.

Photo Credits: © Artush/Shutterstock, cover, 1, 20; © Sergey Rzyhov/Shutterstock, 4; © Jorgefelix | Dreamstime.com, 6; © aksphoto/Thinkstock, 8; © Moizhusein | Dreamstime.com, 10; © Repina Valeriya/Shutterstock, 12; © Kjetil Kolbjornsrud/Shutterstock, 14; © Mogens Trolle/Shutterstock, 16; © Nazzu | Dreamstime.com - Ostriches Photo, 18

Copyright © 2017 by Cherry Lake Publishing
All rights reserved. No part of this book may be reproduced or utilized in any
form or by any means without written permission from the publisher.

Library of Congress Cataloging-in-Publication Data

Names: Cunningham, Kevin, 1966- author.
Title: Zebras and ostriches / Kevin Cunningham.
Description: Ann Arbor, MI : Cherry Lake Publishing, [2016] | Series: Better together |
    Audience: K to grade 3. | Includes bibliographical references and index.
Identifiers: LCCN 2015049441 | ISBN 9781634710824 (hardcover) | ISBN 9781634712804 (pbk.) |
    ISBN 9781634711814 (pdf) | ISBN 9781634713795 (ebook)
Subjects: LCSH: Mutualism (Biology)—Juvenile literature. | Ostriches—Juvenile literature. |
    Zebras—Juvenile literature. | Animal behavior—Juvenile literature.
Classification: LCC QH548.3 .C866 2016 | DDC 591.7/85—dc23
LC record available at http://lccn.loc.gov/2015049441

Cherry Lake Publishing would like to acknowledge the work of The Partnership for 21st Century Skills.
Please visit *www.p21.org* for more information.

Printed in the United States of America
Corporate Graphics

CONTENTS

5 **Big, Big Bird**

9 **Keeping Watch**

13 **Smelling Danger**

17 **Helping Each Other**

22 Glossary

23 Find Out More

24 Index

24 About the Author

Ostrich eggs are huge! Baby ostriches are about 10 inches (25.4 centimeters) tall.

Big, Big Bird

The ostrich is the biggest bird in the world. How big? Some people in Africa ride on its back. The ostrich stands tall. An adult female grows to a height of 5.5 to 6.6 feet (1.7 to 2 meters). Male adults reach between 5.9 and 9 feet (1.8 and 2.7 m) tall. Ostriches lay the biggest eggs. How big? One ostrich egg weighs the same as 24 chicken eggs. The ostrich has the

Ostriches and zebras share a habitat.
They like open spaces with lots of grass.

biggest eye of any land animal. How big? An ostrich's eye is about 1.9 inches (5 centimeters) across.

Big eyes come in handy on Africa's **savanna**. The ostrich's eyes help another animal on the savanna survive. That animal, the plains zebra, returns the favor. Its sense of smell helps the ostrich.

Ask Questions!

A myth is an untrue story. One myth says a scared ostrich hides its head in the ground. Think of a story you have heard about animals. Ask a parent, teacher, librarian, or other adult if the story is true.

A group of ostriches is called a herd.

Keeping Watch

An ostrich's eyes can see far. They also see details very clearly. Ostriches need super eyes. **Predators** like lions and hyenas prowl on the savanna.

Ostriches are **social** animals. They live in groups with one male and many females. All of the females keep their eggs in one giant nest. The male stands guard. He will attack if predators come close

An ostrich has long, strong legs that help him defend his herd and run fast.

to the nest. He kicks hard. An ostrich kick can kill a lion.

Other times, an ostrich runs from predators. Ostriches cannot fly. They have to race away on foot.

Speed gives ostriches an **advantage**. Few animals can keep up with an ostrich. It can run almost 50 miles (80.5 kilometers) per hour. One ostrich **stride** carries the bird from 7.2 to 16 feet (2 to 5 m). But an ostrich cannot just zoom to top speed in one step. It needs a warning.

Zebras are members of the horse family.

Smelling Danger

No two plains zebras have the same stripes. The stripes are a sort of **camouflage**. Plains zebras are social animals. They live in groups. When a group of zebras is attacked, they run. The stripes on one animal blend into the stripes on the next. Predators cannot focus on a single animal, giving the zebras a chance to escape.

Lions, leopards, cheetahs, and hyenas are dangerous predators that share the savanna with zebras.

Predators on the savanna hunt the zebras. Predators use camouflage, too. A plains zebra must stay on guard. Its powerful nose always sniffs the air. It tries to smell predators.

Zebras have good **vision**. But a group could miss a camouflaged predator. That's how the ostrich helps zebras. Ostriches have a poor sense of smell. That's how the zebra helps the ostrich.

Look!

Many animals use camouflage. What animals in your town are hard to see? Why is it hard to see them? Can you think of other animals that use camouflage to hide in snow, trees, or grass?

When a herd of zebras runs from a predator it's called a stampede.

Helping Each Other

Ostriches and plains zebras roam together on the savanna. Each brings advantages. Each makes up part of a team.

The ostrich's sharp vision and height make it good at spotting predators. That adds to the zebra's own ability to see. A plains zebra's nose finds predators. That makes up for the ostrich's poor sense of smell.

By teaming up, they can see and smell even the sneakiest predator.

Both ostriches and zebras use sounds to communicate.

A plains zebra has one more advantage. It **communicates** with other plains zebras. When one smells a predator, it cries out, *kwa-ha, kwa-ha, kwa-ha-ha*. This warning gives the zebra group time to run away. Plains zebras run about 40 miles (64 km) per hour at top speed.

Ostriches know the plains zebra's **alarm** call. When they hear *kwa-ha, kwa-ha, kwa-ha-ha*, they race off, too. Their long strides take them away from predators. Plains zebras also listen for an ostrich's alarm. An ostrich often lets out a hiss when it spots danger. It can also give out a deep grunt.

The savanna is dangerous but the zebra and the ostrich help keep each other safe.

An alarm helps in another way. Imagine ostriches and plains zebras running all over the place. Confusing, right? The predator gets confused, too. Sometimes it chases an animal it cannot catch. Then the predator must rest before hunting again.

The ostriches and plains zebras soon find each other. They settle down to feed. They have survived once more, thanks to teamwork.

Create!

Plains zebras communicate with their faces. Their ears fold down or stand up to show their feelings. Get a piece of paper and colored pencils. Draw three pictures of ways you communicate without words.

GLOSSARY

advantage (ad-VAN-tij) something that helps an animal

alarm (uh-LAHRM) a sound that warns of danger

camouflage (KAM-uh-flahzh) the ways an animal makes itself harder to see

communicates (kuh-MYOO-ni-kates) shares information

predators (PRED-uh-turz) animals that hunt other animals for food

savanna (suh-VAN-uh) a flat, grassy area with few trees

social (SO-shul) living in large groups

stride (STRYD) a long step

vision (VIZH-uhn) eyesight

FIND OUT MORE

BOOKS

Nagelhout, Ryan. *Awesome Ostriches*. New York: Gareth Stevens, 2013.

Raatma, Lucia. *Plains Zebras*. Danbury, CT: Children's Press, 2014.

Schaefer, Lola M., with Paul Meisel. *Run for Your Life! Predators and Prey on the African Savanna*. New York: Holiday House, 2016.

WEB SITES

Dublin Zoo—African Savanna
www.dublinzoo.ie/159/African-Savanna.aspx

National Geographic—Zebra
http://animals.nationalgeographic.com/animals/mammals/zebra

San Diego Zoo—Animals: Zebra
http://animals.sandiegozoo.org/animals/zebra

Toronto Zoo—Ostrich
www.torontozoo.com/explorethezoo/AnimalDetails.asp?pg=619

INDEX

A
alarm call, 19, 21

C
camouflage, 13, 15
communication, 18, 19, 21

D
danger, 13–16, 19

E
eggs, 4, 5, 9

H
habitat, 6
herd, 8

N
nests, 9, 11

O
ostriches
　eyes, 7, 9, 15, 17
　legs, 10
　size, 4, 5
　and zebras, 6, 17–21

P
predators, 9, 11, 13–17, 21

R
running, 10, 11, 19

S
savanna, 7, 14, 15, 20
stampede, 16

Z
zebras, 12–16
　and ostriches, 6, 17–21
　running, 19
　sense of smell, 7, 15, 17

ABOUT THE AUTHOR

Kevin Cunningham is the author of more than 60 books. He lives near Chicago.